ISBN: 9781794331372

Q. What did the little corn say to the mama corn?

A. Where's pop corn?

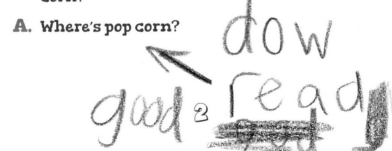

Q. What goes "Ha ha ha.....THUD!"?

A. A monster laughing his head off.

Q. What's green and can fly?

A. Super Pickle!

Q. What is fast, loud and crunchy?

A. A rocket chip!

Q. What is a crocodile's favorite game?

A. Snap!

Q. What's orange and sounds like a parrot?

A. A carrot.

Q. What do elves learn at school?

A. The elf-abet.

Q. What is a toad's favorite drink?

A. Croak-a-cola.

Q. What's a monster's favorite game?

A. Swallow the leader.

Q. Why did the banana go to the doctor?

A. Because he wasn't peeling well

5

Knock Knock

Who's there

Atish

Atish who?

Bless you

Knock knock

Who's there?

Boo

Boo who?

Don't cry its only me.

Q. What do you give a sick bird?

A. Tweetment

Q. What did one snowman say to the other?

A. Can you smell carrots?

Q. What do you call a fairy that doesn't like to wash?

A. Stinkerbell.

Q. What is the martians' favorite party food?

A. Martian-mallows!

Knock knock

Who's there?

Mikey!

Mikey who?

Mikey doesn't fit in the keyhole!

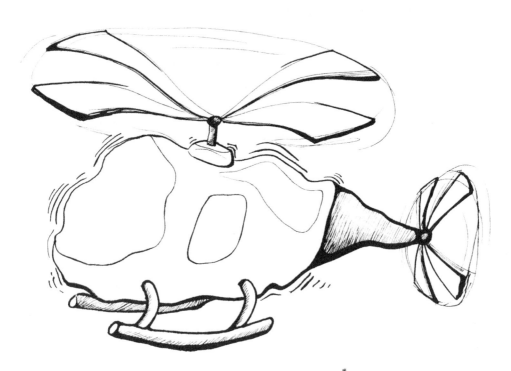

Q. What wobbles in the sky?

A. A Jelly-copter.

do read good

Knock knock

Who's there?

Howard!

Howard who?

Howard I know?

Knock knock

Who's there?

Ice cream!

Ice cream who?

Ice cream if you don't let me in!

Knock knock

Who's there?

Cows!

Cows who?

Cows go 'moo' not who!

Knock knock

Who's there?

Tank!

Tank who?

You're welcome!

Knock knock

Who's there?

Luke!

Luke who?

Luke through the keyhole and you can see!

Knock knock

Who's there?

Wooden shoe!

Wooden shoe who?

Wooden shoe like to hear another joke?

Q. What do kittens like to eat?

A. Mice cream.

11

Q. What did the hat say to the scarf?

A. You hang around, and I'll go ahead.

Q. What do you call a bear in the rain?

A. A Drizzly Bear.

Q. Why did the boy throw the butter out the window?

A. To see a butterfly!

Q. Why does a penguin carry a fish in it's beak?

A. Because it doesn't have any pockets!

Q. What do you call a blind dinosaur?

A. A do-you-think-he-saw-us.

Q. What kind of bees make milk?

A. Boo-bees.

Q. What is the hottest day in summer?

A. Sun-day

Q. What do cows read?

A. Cattle-logs.

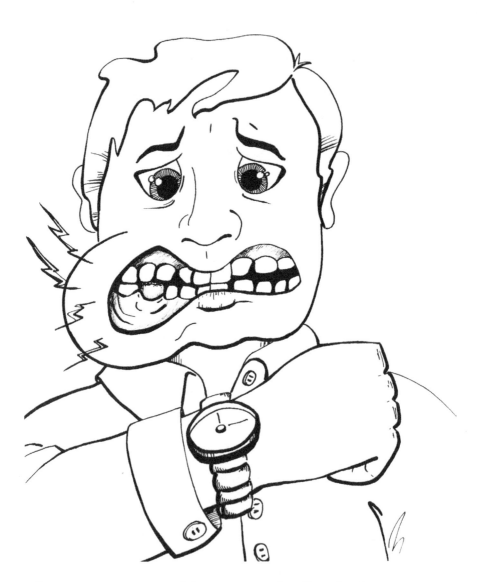

Q. What time should you go to the dentist?

A. Tooth hurty.

don't read Boring

14

Q. What did the policeman say to his tummy?

A. Freeze. You're under a vest.

Q. What do you call a rich elf?

A. Welfy.

Q. What do you call Santa on a break?

A. Santa Pause!

Q. Why was the broom late?

A. It over swept!

Q. What did the horse say when it fell?

A. I've fallen and I can't giddyup!

Q. What kind of button is impossible to undo?

A. Your belly button.

Q. Why was six afraid of seven?

A. Because seven eight nine.

Q. Why are fish so smart?

A. Because they live in schools.

Q. What do gorillas sing at Christmas?

A. 'Jungle bells, jungle bells!'

Q. What animal can you always find at a baseball game?

A. A bat.

Q. What do you get if you sit under a cow.

A. A pat on the head

Q. What did the nose say to the finger?

A. Quit picking on me!

Q. Why didn't the skeleton go to the dance?

A. He had no body to dance with.

Q. What kind of hair do oceans have?

A. Wavy.

Q. Why didn't the orange win the race?

A. It ran out of juice.

Q. What flies around the school at night?

A. The alpha-bat

Q. Where do baby apes sleep?

A. In apricots.

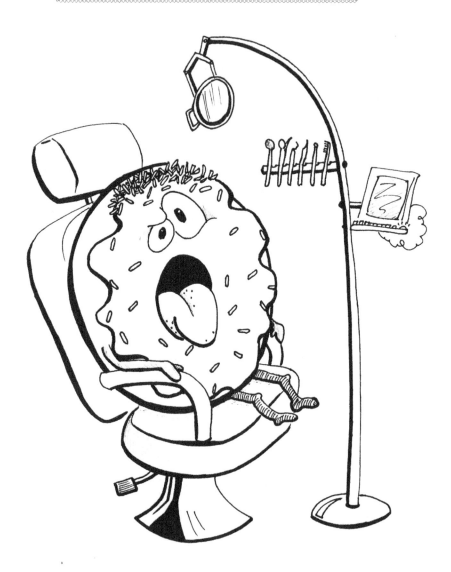

Q. Why did the donut go to the dentist?

A. To get a filling.

do read good

20

Q. How does a lion greet the other animals in the field?

A. Pleased to eat you!

Q. What is a cat's favorite color?

A. Purrr-ple

Q. What kind of key opens a banana

A. A mon-key

Q. Why do giraffes have long necks?

A. Because they have smelly feet!

Q. Why did the children eat their homework?

A. Because their teacher said it was a piece of cake.

Q. How does a train sneeze?

A. ah-choo-choo.

Q. Why did the new boy steal a chair from the classroom?

A. Because the teacher told him to take a seat.

Q. What kind of beans can't grow in a garden?

A. Jelly beans!

Q. Why did the elephant paint its toenails red?

A. So it could hide in a cherry tree.

Q. What do you call a boy with a dictionary in his pocket?

A. Smartie Pants!

Q. Where do ghosts go to post letters?

A. At the ghost office

Q. What is a horse's favorite sport?

A. Stable tennis!

Q. How do you count cows?

A. With a cowculator.

Q. Why did the bunny go to the hospital?

A. For a hoperation.

Q. Where do rabbits go after their wedding?

A. On their bunnymoon!

Q. Why was the crab sent to prison?

A. Because he kept pinching things!

Q. How does a mouse feel after taking a shower?

A. Squeaky-clean!

Q. How much fur can you get from a werewolf?

A. As fur away as possible!

Q. Where do cows go on vacation?

A. Moo York!

Q. What's big, purple and smells horrible

A. A monster's bottom!

Q. Why did the boy sit on his watch?

A. Because he wanted to be on time.

Q. What do you call a bear that is cold?

A. A burr.

Q. Why do hummingbirds hum?

A. Because they don't know the words.

Q. How do you know that carrots are good for your eyes

A. You never see a rabbit wears glasses.

Q. What kind of music are balloons afraid of?

A. Pop music.

Q. Where do you put barking dogs?

A. In a barking lot.

Q. What is a monkeys favorite cookie

A. Chocolate Chimp

don't read Boring

Q. What do you call a baby bear with no teeth?

A. A gummy bear!

Q. What do you call an exploding monkey?

A. A baboom!

Q. What is the difference between a car and a bull?

A. A car only has one horn.

Q. How do you get a dog to stop digging in the garden?

A. Take away his shovel!

Q. What do you call a sheep with no legs?

A. A cloud.

Q. What kind of apple isn't an apple?

A. A pineapple.

Q. Why are elephants wrinkled?

A. Because they don't fit on a ironing board!

Q. What game do elephants play when riding in the back of a car?

A. Squash!

Q. What do you call a shoe made from a banana?

A. A slipper

Q. What color is a burp?

A. Burple.

Q. What happened when the owl lost his voice?

A. He didn't give a hoot!

Q. How do bees get to school?

A. By school buzz!

Q. What do you give an elephant that's going to be sick?

A. Plenty of space!

Q. What kind of bees eat brains?

A. Zombees

Q. What did the horse say when it fell?

A. I've fallen and I can't giddyup!

Q. Why do shepherds never learn to count?

A. Because if they did they would always be falling asleep.

Q. What is a lion's favorite food?

A. Baked beings.

Q. Why did the man burn his ear?

A. He answered the iron!

Q. What clothes should you wear in a storm?

A. Thunderpants.

Q. What do you call a pig that does karate?

A. Pork-Chop!

Q. How do witches style their hair?

A. With scare-spray.

Q. Where do fish save their money?

A. In the river bank!

Q. What did the frog say when he had finished his book?

A. Read it!

Q. What's the biggest mouse in the world?

A. Hippoptamouse

Knock Knock.

Who's there?

Isabel.

Isabel Who?

Isabel working? I've been ringing it for hours!

Q. What is a cats favorite button on a remote?

A. The paws button.

do read good

38

Q. What is the best thing to put in a pie?

A. Your teeth!

Q. What is green and hangs from trees.

A. Giraffe snot.

Q. What so you call a baby insect?

A. A baby buggy!

Q. What is the difference between a bird and fly?

A. A bird can fly but a fly can't bird!

Q. What kind of building has the most stories?

A. The library!

Q. Why did the skeleton go to the barbecue?

A. Because he wanted some spare ribs.

Q. What do you call a train full of chewing gum

A. A chew chew train

Q. Why don't people eat clowns?

A. Because they taste funny!

Q. What bird steals the soap from your bath?

A. A robber duck

do read good

Q. Where does a sheep go to get a haircut?

A. The Baaa-Baaa Shop!

Q. How do you know there's an elephant in your fridge?

A. You can't shut the door!

Q. Why did the girl bring a ruler to bed?

A. Because she wanted to see how long she slept!

Q. Why was the detective at the beach?

A. There was a crime wave!

Q. Why did the policeman have a blanket over himself?

A. He was working undercover!

Q. Which 4 letters frighten a thief?

A. O i c u!

Q. Which jam does a policeman use on his bread?

A. Traffic jam!

Q. What kind of treat do they feed people in prison?

A. Jail- y donuts.

Q. What do sea monsters eat?

A. Fish and ships.

don't
read
Boring

Q. What's a police officers favorite food?

A. Corn on the cop!

Q. What did Mr. and Mrs. Hamburger name their daughter?

A. Patty

Q. What did the square say to the old circle?

A. Been around long?

Q. What kind of snack do you have during a scary movie?

A. I scream

Q. Which runs faster, hot or cold?

A. Hot. Everyone can catch a cold.

Q. What did the stamp say to the envelope?

A. Stick with me we'll go places!

Q. What has hands but does not clap

A. A clock!

Q. What did the math book tell the pencil?

A. I have a lot of problems.

do read good

46

Q. What happens when you tell an egg a joke?

A. It cracks up!!

Q. What did the bunny say on January 1st?

A. Hoppy new year!

Q. Where did the spaghetti go to dance?

A. The Meat Ball!

Q. What is a math teacher's favorite time of year?

A. Summer!

Q. Why is a lost Dalmatian easily found?

A. Because he is always spotted!

Q. What goes tick-tock, woof-woof?

A. A watchdog!

Q. What did the girl sea say when the boy sea asked her for a date?

A. Shore

Q. Why do fish swim in salt water?

A. Pepper makes them sneeze.

Knock Knock. Who's there?

Dishes

Dishes who?

Dishes the police, come out with your hands up!!

Q. Why won't the elephant use the computer?

A. He's afraid of the mouse!

do read good

50

Q. What letters are not in the alphabet?

A. The ones in the mail.

Q. What always falls and never gets hurt?

A. Rain!

Q. What do you call a bird that is sad?

A. A Blue Bird!

Q. What is a pokemon's favorite dance?

A. The hokey pokemon

Q. What is a construction workers favorite bird?

A. A crane!

Q. What lid do you shut every night?

A. Your eyelids.

Q. How did the barber win the race?

A. He took a short cut.

Q. What do you call a teacher with no arms, no legs, and no body?

A. The Head

Q. Why are Teddy Bears never hungry?

A. Because they are always stuffed!

Q. What do you call an old snowman?

A. Water!

Doctor! Doctor! I keep thinking I'm a dog.

Do take a seat

I can't I'm not allowed on the furniture

Q. Why are pirates pirates?

A. Because they Arrrrrrrrrrrr

Q. How do you catch a squirrel?

A. Climb up a tree and act like a nut.

Q. Did you hear about the magic tractor?

A. It turned into a field.

Q. What happens when you give cows lemons?

A. They make lem-moooo-nade!

Q. What do icebergs eat?

A. Iceburgers.

Knock Knock.

Who's there?

Lettuce.

Lettuce who?

Lettuce in, it's freezing out here!

Q. What do a chicken and a band have in common?

A. They both have drum sticks!

don't read Bad

Knock, knock.

Who's there?

Cows go.

Cows go who?

No, silly. Cows go "moo!"

Knock, knock.

Who's there?

Ash.

Ash who?

Bless you!

Knock, knock.

Who's there?

Figs.

Figs who?

Fix your doorbell, it's broken!

Knock, knock.

Who's there?

Pizza.

Pizza who?

Pizza really great guy!

Knock, knock.

Who's there?

Interrupting, squawking parrot.

Interrupting, squawking parr-

SQUAAAAAAAAAWK!

Knock, knock.

Who's there?

Mustache.

Mustache who?

I mustache you a question, but I'll shave it for later.

Q. What kind of cat likes water?

A. An octopuss!

Q. What is black and white and goes round and round?

A. A penguin in a tumble dryer.

Q. Why did the ghost blow his nose?

A. Because it was full of booo-gers!

Q. What is big, green and plays a lot of tricks?

A. Prank-enstein!

Q. Who did the zombie take to the prom?

A. His ghoul-friend!

Q. What did one toilet say to the other?

Q. You look a bit flushed!

Q. Why did the melon jump into the lake?

A. It wanted to be a water-melon.

Q. Why did the cookie go to the doctor?

A. It was feeling crumb-y.

Knock knock.

Who's there?

Nanna.

Nanna who?

Nanna your business, that's who.

Q. What do ghosts use to clean their hair?

A. Sham-boo

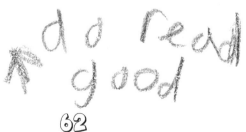

Q. What did the tree say to the wind?

A. Leaf me alone!

Q. How do you know when the moon has had enough to eat?

A. When it's full!

Q. What's a snake's favorite subject?

A. Hisstory.

Q. Why did the egg get thrown out of class?

A. Because he kept telling yolks!

Q. Where do cows go on a Saturday night?

A. To the MOOOOOOOOOOOOOooooooooooovies

Q. What did one plate say to the other plate?

A. Dinner is on me!

Q. What is brown, hairy and wears sunglasses?

A. A coconut on vacation.

Q. How do you stop an astronaut's baby from crying?

A. You rocket!

Q. Did you hear about the man who dreamed he was eating a marshmallow?

A. He woke up and his pillow was gone!

Q. What is a witch's favorite subject in school?

A. Spelling!

Q. Why was the baby strawberry crying?

A. Because her mom and dad were in a jam.

Q. What was the first animal in space?

A. The cow that jumped over the moon

Q. Why did the beach blush?

A. 'Cos the sea wee'd

Q. What starts with E, ends with E, and has only 1 letter in it?

A. Envelope.

Q. If you have 8 apples in one hand and 6 oranges in the other, what do you have?

A. Big hands.

Q. Why did the apple run away?

A. Because the banana split!

Q. What did the beaver say to the tree?

A. "It's been nice gnawing you!"

don't
read
Boring

Q. What goes "thump thump thump squish"?

A. An elephant with a wet tennis shoe.

Q. Why did the girl smear peanut butter on the road?

A. To go with the traffic jam!

Q. Which flower talks the most?

A. Tulips, of course, because they have two lips!

Q. What kind of lion never roars?

A. A dandelion!

Q. What do you get if you cross a frog with a rabbit?

A. A bunny ribbit.

Q. How do you start a teddy bear race?

A. Ready teddy go!

Q. What did 0 say to 8?

A. Nice belt!

Q. What gets wetter the more it dries?

A. A towel!

Q. What did the boy bury his flashlight?

A. Because the battery died!

Q. What has to be broken before you can use it?

A. An egg!

Q. Where does Santa stay when he is on vacation?

A. In a ho-ho-hotel!

Q. What is the biggest ant in the world?

A. An elephant!

Q. Why do gorillas have big nostrils?

A. Because they have big fingers!

Knock knock.

Who's there?

Annie.

Annie who?

Annie way you can let me in soon?

Knock knock.

Who's there?

Stopwatch.

Stopwatch who?

Stopwatch you're doing and pay attention!

Q. What did the bus driver say to the frog?

A. Hop on!

Knock Knock

Who's there

Harry

Harry who?

Harry up and let me in, I'm freezing.

Made in the USA
Monee, IL
11 January 2021